SEASON OF CAROLS

for SOLO VIOLIN and PIANO

Arranged by Bruce Healey

ISBN 0-634-08978-1

HAL•LEONARD® CORPORATION
7777 W. BLUEMOUND RD. P.O.BOX 13819 MILWAUKEE, WI 53213

Visit Hal Leonard Online at
www.halleonard.com

FORWARD AND PERFORMANCE NOTES

The idea behind the creation of these arrangements is to provide music that would be performable by student musicians who have studied string instruments for at least one year. Equally important is to provide interesting high quality arrangements of popular traditional holiday songs with a level of musical sophistication not often found in student literature. This effort has resulted in material that could be programmed by professional players as well.

Each piece has challenges which align with studies and techniques a student player encounters in popular second and third year string educational programs.

• FINGERINGS:
The vast majority of the violin parts can be performed in 1st position, if needed. I have marked many 1st position fingerings as helpful reminders for the student and as aids to the teacher. At times a passage may require shifts to other positions, or be more playable and should better in other positions, but I have given optional notes for 1st position playing where necessary.

• BOWINGS:
The bowings have been marked as a starting point. To a certain extent, take into consideration the young students' lesser bow control. There are, of course, other possibilities for bowings depending on the ability of the players and the desired musical result.

• POSSIBILITIES FOR PEDAGOGY:
All of these pieces contain the opportunity to explore dynamics. They also have harmonic content that is a bit sophisticated and, in that way, can be opportunities to focus on intonation.

Away In A Manger: Legato bowing; bow control.

Deck The Hall: Playing off the string, playing marcato.

Ding Dong! Merrily On High!: "Bell Tones" *fp*; staccato; intonation.

Greensleeves: Many optional positions; legato bowing; expression; balance.

God Rest Ye Merry, Gentlemen: Tempo changes; off the string; optional double bow strokes.

O Come, All Ye Faithful: Tonalization; dynamics.

Chanukah, Oy Chanukah: Easy optional double stops; bowing.

O Holy Night: Bowing; simple duplets in 6/8; slightly chromatic harmony.

Pat-A-Pan: Probably the most challenging piece in the collection; key of G minor introduces "Lo 1" fingering for B♭ and E♭; key change to A minor.

Silent Night: Bow control.

Three Holiday Songs: Pizzicato section can be bowed if desired.

We Wish You A Merry Christmas: "Bell tones" *fp*; key change from G major to D major.

I'd especially like to thank Gail Acosta, David Killen and Nancy Schindler for kindly reviewing the pieces and making helpful suggestions.

Bruce Healey

SEASON OF CAROLS is also available for:
Solo Viola and Piano......00842194
Solo Cello and Piano......00842195
String Quartet..................04490404

String Orchestra

Conductor....04490308
Violin 1.........04490309
Violin 2........ 04490310
Violin 3 (opt.)....04490311
Viola..................04490312
String Bass.........04490314
Piano...................... 04490315
Harp (opt.).............04490316
Percussion (opt.)....04490317

DECK THE HALL

Traditional Welsh Carol
Arranged by BRUCE HEALEY

Allegretto (𝅗𝅥 = 88)

f marcato
f marcato
26
(4)
35
mf legato
mf legato
31
f marcato
f marcato
(4)
37
43
(4)
fp
f

AWAY IN A MANGER

Traditional
Words by JOHN T. McFARLAND (v.3)
Music by JAMES R. MURRAY
Arranged by BRUCE HEALEY

24
hi 2
mf
sim.
Ped.
23
32
28
3rd pos.
34
41
p
1st pos.
rit.
vibrato
40

GREENSLEEVES

16th Century Traditional English
Arranged by BRUCE HEALEY

21
1st pos.
mf
p
26
vibrato
3rd pos.
29
mf
31
mp
35
2nd pos.
37
mf
1st pos.

vibrato
port.
3rd pos.
39
45
f
43
48
rit.
(1st pos. 8vb opt.)
p
save bow
52

GOD REST YE MERRY, GENTLEMEN

19th Century English Carol
Arranged by BRUCE HEALEY

24
31
lo 1
30
lo 1
fp
fp
36
43
(double-strokes opt.)
hi 3
lo 2
f
f
42

51
hi 3
48
59
3rd pos.
1st pos.
3rd pos.
54
60
accel.
1st pos.
ff
accel.
ff
66

73
Boldly (𝅗𝅥 = 128)
81
f (full bow)
f
molto rit.
molto rit.
Slower (♩ = 112)
sfz
f
mp
mp
rit.
rit.
mf

O COME, ALL YE FAITHFUL

(Adeste Fideles)

Words and Music by JOHN FRANCIS WADE
Latin Words translated by FREDERICK OAKELEY
Arranged by BRUCE HEALEY

Moderato (♩ = 108)

00841986

21
mf
mf
18
Ped.
Ped.
22
Ped.
Ped.
Ped.
Ped.
Ped.
Ped.
sim.
29
f
f
26
33
p
p
30

mp
3rd pos.
f
34
41
piu f
38
rit.
42

SILENT NIGHT

Words by JOSEPH MOHR
Translated by JOHN F. YOUNG
Music by FRANZ X. GRUBER
Arranged by BRUCE HEALEY

18
21
Ped.
23
mf dim.
mf
29
warmly
pp
mp
poco cresc.
28
33
37

38
Ped.
45
43
48
mf
mp
(4)
(frog)
rit. e dim.
rit. e dim.

DING DONG! MERRILY ON HIGH!

French Carol
Arranged by BRUCE HEALEY

24
f
29
mp
hi 3
(4)
34
37
mf
0
39
3rd pos.
1st pos.
43

DECK THE HALL

SOLO VIOLIN

Traditional Welsh Carol
Arranged by BRUCE HEALEY

00841986

AWAY IN A MANGER

SOLO VIOLIN

Traditional
Words by JOHN T. McFARLAND (v.3)
Music by JAMES R. MURRAY
Arranged by BRUCE HEALEY

GREENSLEEVES

SOLO VIOLIN

16th Century Traditional English
Arranged by BRUCE HEALEY

00841986

GOD REST YE MERRY, GENTLEMEN

SOLO VIOLIN

19th Century English Carol
Arranged by BRUCE HEALEY

51
47
hi 3
3rd pos.
52
59
1st pos.
3rd pos.
57
63
accel.
1st pos.
ff
68
73 Boldly
2
73
81
2
f
(full bow)
78
molto rit.
83
Slower
sfz
88
f
mp
rit.
93

O COME, ALL YE FAITHFUL
(Adeste Fideles)

SOLO VIOLIN

Words and Music by JOHN FRANCIS WADE
Latin Words translated by FREDERICK OAKELEY
Arranged by BRUCE HEALEY

SILENT NIGHT

SOLO VIOLIN

Words by JOSEPH MOHR
Translated by JOHN F. YOUNG
Music by FRANZ X. GRUBER
Arranged by BRUCE HEALEY

DING DONG! MERRILY ON HIGH!

SOLO VIOLIN

French Carol
Arranged by BRUCE HEALEY

00841986

hi 3
49
f
hi 3
p
cresc.
57
f
65
3rd pos.
1st pos.
1.
2.
fp
(4)
f

CHANUKAH, OY CHANUKAH

SOLO VIOLIN

Traditional Hebrew Lyrics
Chanukah Melody
Arranged by BRUCE HEALEY

00841986

35
40
45
49
53
55
58
62
3rd pos.
mp
cresc.
1st pos.
3rd pos.
hi3
(Opt. 8vb to end)
4th pos.
1st pos.
hi3

PAT-A-PAN
(Willie, Take Your Little Drum)

SOLO VIOLIN

Words and Music by BERNARD de la MONNOYE
Arranged by BRUCE HEALEY

O HOLY NIGHT

SOLO VIOLIN

French Words by PLACIDE CAPPEAU
English Words by JOHN S. DWIGHT
Music by ADOLPHE ADAM
Arranged by BRUCE HEALEY

THREE HOLIDAY SONGS

(The Dreydl Song • Jingle Bells • Joy To The World)

SOLO VIOLIN

Arranged by BRUCE HEALEY

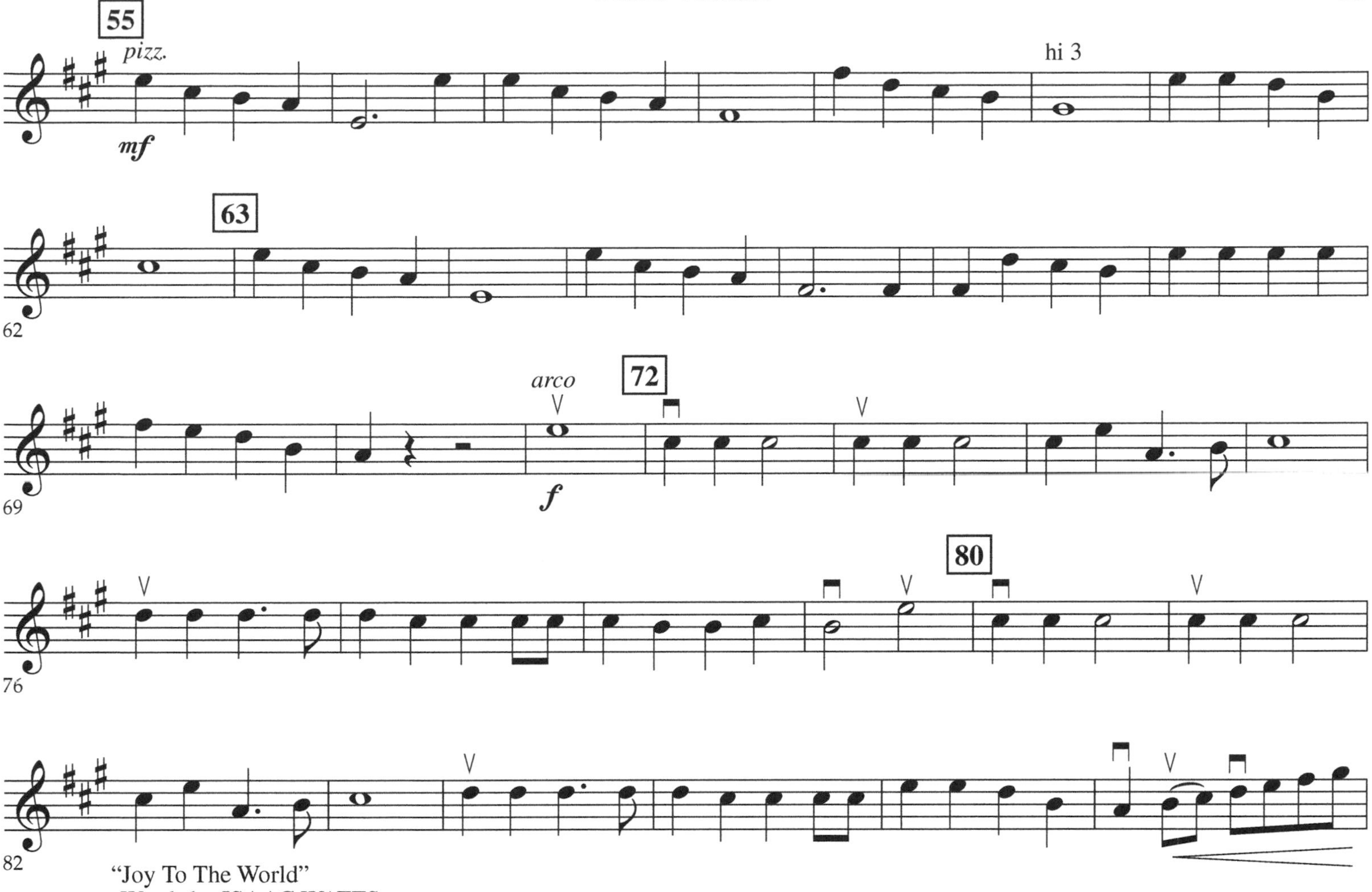

"Joy To The World"
Words by ISAAC WATTS
Music by GEORGE FRIDERIC HANDEL

WE WISH YOU A MERRY CHRISTMAS

SOLO VIOLIN

Traditional English Folksong
Arranged by BRUCE HEALEY

00841986

hi 3
4
44
49
f
hi 3
4
3
p
57
cresc.
f
54
59

65
8va
2nd time
3rd pos.
64
1st pos.
(8va)
1.
68
2.
fp
(4)
73
f
78

CHANUKAH, OY CHANUKAH

Traditional Hebrew Lyrics
Chanukah Melody
Arranged by BRUCE HEALEY

00841986

18
Subito faster (♩ = 144)
(V)
24
p
mf
22
26
(hold 1)
34
30

35
39
45
43
47

51
3rd pos.
55
mp cresc.
1st pos.
mp cresc.
3rd pos.
hi3
(Opt. 8vb to end)
59
63
4th pos.
1st pos.
hi3

PAT-A-PAN

(Willie, Take Your Little Drum)

Words and Music by BERNARD de la MONNOYE
Arranged by BRUCE HEALEY

26
33
mf marcato
mf marcato
lo 2
32
lo 2
lo 1
lo 2
2
43
lo 1
mf
39
lo 1
45

hi 3
53
f marcato
lo 2
51
hi 3
56
64
piu f
hi 3
62
68
2

O HOLY NIGHT

French Words by PLACIDE CAPPEAU
English Words by JOHN S. DWIGHT
Music by ADOLPHE ADAM
Arranged by BRUCE HEALEY

21
29
37
f
Ped.
21
26
31
36

mp
mf
41
lo 2
f
p
rit. (2nd time)
1.
save bow
46
2.
a tempo
52
rit. e dim.
58

THREE HOLIDAY SONGS
(The Dreydl Song • Jingle Bells • Joy To The World)

"The Dreydl Song"
Traditional

Arranged by BRUCE HEALEY

Allegro (𝅗𝅥 = 112)

23 "Jingle Bells"
Words and Music by J. PIERPONT

47
pizz.
mf
p
55
53
hi 3
63
59
arco
f
65

72
mf
80
78
"Joy To The World"
Words by ISAAC WATTS
Music by GEORGE FRIDERIC HANDEL
f
84
95
90

99
pp
mp
96
f
1.
102
2.
108
107
112

WE WISH YOU A MERRY CHRISTMAS

Traditional English Folksong
Arranged by BRUCE HEALEY

28
mf
mf
24
Ped. sim.
29
36
34
43
mf
40

46
51
mf
hi 3
51
59
legato
legato
56
67
f marc.
f marc.
62

68
73
77
fp
fp
fp
fp
78
fp
fp
fp
4
p
cresc.
p
cresc.
83
f
rit.
f
rit.